Thank you!

for your purchase
and
for supporting us

If you love our product or have any suggestions, we'd be very grateful for your review!

Manufactured by Amazon.ca
Bolton, ON

19833155R00026